LONG LOAN

Witness History Series

TOWARDS EUROPEAN UNITY

Stewart Ross

Wayland

Titles in this series:

The Arab–Israeli Conflict
China since 1945
The Cold War
The Origins of the First World War
The Russian Revolution
South Africa since 1948
The Third Reich
Towards European Unity
The United Nations
The USA since 1945

First published in 1989 by
Wayland (Publishers) Ltd
61 Western Road, Hove
East Sussex BN3 1JD, England

© Copyright 1989 Wayland (Publishers) Ltd

Editor: Susannah Foreman
Series editor: Catherine Ellis
Consultant: Derek Heater, freelance writer
Designer: Ross George

British Library Cataloguing in Publication Data
Ross, Stewart
    Towards European unity. – (Witness history series).
    1. European community countries. Integration
    I. Title II. Series
    337.1'42

ISBN 1–85210–812–6

Phototypeset by Kalligraphics Limited, Horley, Surrey
Printed and bound by Sagdos, S.p.A., Milan

Contents

1
INTRODUCTION
Peoples and countries

HAVE YOU EVER CONSIDERED what a country is? It is a number of people who live together under the same government in a clearly defined territory. They do not all necessarily speak the same language, or follow the same religion, or even have very similar cultures. And countries are not permanent. Following the First World War two new European countries were created, Czechoslovakia and Yugoslavia. Long ago Wessex, Kent, Mercia, Northumbria and Cumbria were once separate English kingdoms. Scotland became part of the United Kingdom less than 300 years ago, while Germany and Italy have been in existence for scarcely more than a century.

Yet, despite the fact that the inhabitants of a country do not always have much in common, and countries have been made

The peoples of the world are always on the move, so no country contains just one racial type. In the UK the Celts and Saxons have been joined by people from Asia, Africa and the Caribbean.

and unmade over the centuries, people become passionately devoted to their home-land. People become irrationally angry when their native land is criticized. This powerful feeling is known as patriotism, or nationalism. Sometimes, as when it inspires writers or artists, it can be a very creative force. The Polish composer Chopin, for example, wrote much of his brilliant piano music when fired by love for his country.

On the other hand, nationalism can be a terribly destructive force. It can encourage an illogical dislike of foreigners, or blindness towards the faults of one's own country.

This can lead to the sort of violent behaviour seen among the crowds at football matches between teams from different countries. An extreme example of this occurred in 1985 at the Heysel Stadium, Brussels, when 41 people died before a match between the Italian team Juventus and Liverpool.

Even more tragically, almost all modern wars grow out of disputes between countries. No group of countries has been more at fault in this than those of Europe. Both the First and Second World Wars began as European conflicts.

Therefore, in the same way as the separate states that made up Germany came together to form one country in 1871, since 1945 there has been a concerted effort to bring the countries of Europe closer together. A community has been created. Perhaps, in the future, it will grow into a totally new country: Europe.

Pride in one's country can lead to a healthy desire to maintain traditional culture (above). But nationalism also gives rise to hatred of 'outsiders', shown at its worst by Nazi attacks on Jews during the 1930s (below).

2
THE LESSONS OF HISTORY
Empires and ideas

A page from a fourteenth-century Bible. Throughout the Middle Ages all Europe was seen as part of Christendom. The Church, using Latin as an international language, provided Europe with a powerful common culture.

THE PRESENT MAP OF Europe, divided into many small countries, is quite new. In prehistoric times there were no national boundaries at all. Then, between the first century BC and the fifth century AD, the Romans carved out a huge empire that took in about half of Europe as well as much of north Africa and the Middle East.

Although the Roman Empire, with its common currency, law and government, collapsed, memories of its grandeur still lived on. In AD 800, Charles the Great (Charlemagne), who ruled a territory that included France, northern Italy, Switzerland and much of Germany and Austria, had himself crowned Holy Roman Emperor. This title, although it soon did not mean very much, survived until the time of Napoleon. Moreover, until the Reformation in the sixteenth century, all Western Europe belonged to the same powerful Catholic Church, controlled by the Pope in Rome. This Church, with its own law and common language, Latin, was truly international, so the idea of a common European culture was kept alive.

Intellectuals also dreamed of a united Europe. In his book *The Monarchia* (c. 1309), the Italian writer Dante urged 'a unique princedom extending over all persons in time'.[1] Dante, and his influential contemporary, Marsiglio of Padua, were looking for ways of maintaining peace in Europe. Three hundred years later the great French minister, the Duke of Sully, wrote about a grand design for the same end:

> ...the affairs of Europe were to be regulated by seven general councils, of which six were local, and the seventh, meeting in some city of central Europe, was to decide questions of common interest... Disarmament was to be general; control of a composite army, to which each state would contribute, was to be in the hands of the Supreme Council.[2]

The Napoleonic Empire.

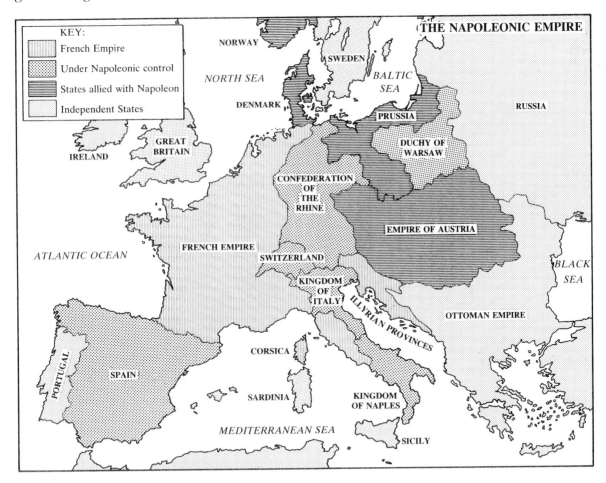

KEY:
- French Empire
- Under Napoleonic control
- States allied with Napoleon
- Independent States

THE NAPOLEONIC EMPIRE

For a brief while at the beginning of the nineteenth century the brilliant French general, Napoleon Bonaparte, conquered an empire that stretched from Naples and Seville in the south, to the Baltic in the north. You can see on the map above the full extent of Napoleon's vast empire. But, like previous attempts at European unity based on conquest, the empire did not last. If the path to permanent peace lay through unity, then that unity had to come through agreement, not war.

The horror of war

After the Napoleonic Wars, the great powers of Europe met together in Vienna to create a lasting peace. Their thinking was based upon the idea of a 'balance of power', with no one state having control, and meetings (congresses) between the larger states. Although there was no major European conflict for a while, in the end the system collapsed. A wave of nationalism was sweeping the continent, leading to the formation of new countries. Some of these, such as Serbia, were small, but the creation of others, such as Germany and Italy, altered the existing balance of European power. National rivalries abounded. Finally, in the summer of 1914 Europe plunged into full-scale war. Such was the influence of the European states, with their overseas empires and gigantic navies, that the whole world was soon involved.

The First World War became known as the 'war to end all wars'. Its terrible slaughter and destruction horrified the leaders of all nations, but particularly those of Europe, where most of the fighting had taken place. A League of Nations was established in Geneva after the war, and disarmament was considered. Two of the leading figures in this drive towards greater understanding were Aristide Briand, the French Prime Minister, and Gustav Stresemann, the German Foreign Minister. In 1926 they were jointly awarded the Nobel Peace Prize for trying to bring their countries together. Another influential figure was Count Richard Coudenhove-Kalergi who founded

Berlin families search for fuel. Economic hardship led millions of Germans to accept Hitler's extreme racialist and nationalist views.

Gustav Stresemann (left) and Aristide Briand (above). In the 1920s these men worked to bring their countries to close political union. Might their efforts have lasted longer if they had worked for closer economic co-operation?

The hard-pressed people were demanding a way out of their sorry predicament. The millions of unemployed wanted jobs. The shopkeepers wanted help... To all the millions of discontented Hitler... offered what seemed to them, in their misery, some measure of hope.[3]

a Pan-European Union after the war. In his book *Paneuropa* (1923), he urged the states of Europe to share common economic and foreign policies. To some extent these men were the heirs of the ideas for European unity first expressed by Dante and Sully.

However, the links created between nations in the 1920s were political, not economic. So, when a world-wide economic slump began in 1929, national rivalries re-emerged. In Germany in 1930:

In 1933, Adolf Hitler, with his dreams of creating an empire from the English Channel to the Ural mountains, became Chancellor of Germany. Six years later the flimsy mechanisms of peace had been swept aside. Yet again the people of Europe found themselves at the heart of terrible, total war.

3
THE BIRTH OF THE COMMUNITY
Post-war Europe

IN 1945 THE CONTINENT of Europe was shattered. Some commentators thought that it would never recover from the effects of the Second World War. These effects can be examined under four headings:

Personal suffering. Millions of soldiers and civilians had been killed in the fighting. It is estimated that the Germans lost about 3,250,000 soldiers, while some 60,000 citizens had been killed in the city of Dresden alone when it was razed to the ground by allied bombing in February 1945. Other warring nations had suffered terrible losses, but, apart from the USSR, which lost 20 million people, not on the same scale as

Bremen after wartime bombing. Why do you think the founders of the EC believed that reconciliation between former enemies was as important as reconstruction?

Germany. Bitter hatred remained. It is said that when the allied forces freed France about 40,000 French people were executed for collaborating with the Germans. Millions were homeless. Refugees thronged the streets, highways and shelters.

Physical destruction. All over Europe houses, factories and offices had been smashed by bombing and ground fighting. Communications were broken, owing to cut telephone wires, fractured bridges, railway lines and roads. Food and medicine were in desperately short supply.

Colonial unrest. A good deal of Europe's prosperity over the previous century had come through trade on favourable terms with its world-wide empires. Now, led by powerful states such as India, these colonies were demanding independence from their European masters.

Loss of power. As an official EC booklet puts it:

The only real victors in this European Civil War [the Second World War] are the United States and the Soviet Union. The two great powers, each profoundly convinced of the inherent superiority of its own ideology, dominate the world and its immediate future.[4]

In Zurich, Switzerland, on 19 September 1945, the British statesman Winston Churchill declared:

Winston Churchill, whose 1945 speech is seen as one of the milestones on the route to European unity.

We must build a kind of United States of Europe… Time may be short. At present there is a breathing space, but if we are to form a united states of Europe – or whatever name it may take – then we must begin now. I say to you: Let it arise.[5]

Look carefully at the four problems outlined above. How do you think that the establishment of a United States of Europe would help to solve them?

By 1946 it was clear that mutual suspicion and fear separated Soviet-dominated Eastern Europe from the democratic states in the West. In 1948, under what was known as the Marshall Plan, the USA began pouring aid into Western Europe to speed its economic recovery enabling it to resist the threat of communism. One condition of this aid was that the recipient nations administered it among themselves. To do this the Organization for European Economic Co-operation (OEEC) was established by representatives of the governments concerned. The first small but significant step had been taken towards Churchill's 'United States'.

The ECSC

More than ten years elapsed between Churchill's famous speech calling for a United States of Europe and the formation of the EEC. In the years between, as well as the foundation of the OEEC, there was an important step forward but also a painful step back on the path to unity.

On 9 May 1950, the French Foreign Minister Robert Schuman proposed, 'It is no longer the moment for vain words, but for a bold act – a constructive act'.[6] His suggestion, which had been first put forward by the French economist Jean Monnet (at that time his country's National Plan Commissioner), was that France and Germany should pool their production and consumption of coal and steel. All European countries were free to join the new organization.

One of the major steel and coal producing areas of France was Alsace-Lorraine. In 1871 these provinces had been seized from France by Germany; in 1918 they reverted

to France, only to be re-occupied by the Germans in 1940. In 1945 they became part of France once more. Do you think that it was significant that Schuman lived in Lorraine?

In April 1951 the European Coal and Steel Community (ECSC) came into being. France and Germany were joined by Italy, Belgium, the Netherlands and Luxembourg, known collectively as the Six. In one very important respect the ECSC was an entirely new concept. The Six did not just co-operate together to direct the ECSC, they set up a High Authority, comprising members from all the ECSC states, but with its own independent power. Thus was created a truly European governmental organization to which all national governments of the Six handed

Jean Monnet (right), the French economist who is seen as the founder of the ECSC. He believed in the importance of European economic co-operation. He is seen here with Henry Kissinger.

In 1948 the Soviets established a blockade of West Berlin, and intensified the Cold War. In response a European Defence Community was proposed.

over some of their sovereign power. The ECSC also had a Council of Ministers, a Court of Justice and an Assembly. The powers of the High Authority were clearly limited, but it could be seen as the first step towards a government for a United States of Europe.

Encouraged by the success of the ECSC, and anxious about the growing tension between democratic Western Europe and the communist East, the Six sought closer unity. In 1952 it was proposed to merge the Community's armed forces into a European Defence Community (EDC). At the same time it was proposed that a European Political Community would be given much greater political powers over the individual six states, particularly in foreign affairs. This plan was too radical; at the end of August 1954 it was rejected.

Why was the EC formed?

Undaunted by the failure of the EDC, ministers of the Six met at Messina in Italy in 1955 to discuss further economic co-operation. A committee was established under the chairmanship of the Belgian Foreign Minister, Paul-Henri Spaak, to come up with some proposals. Just under a year later, the ministers met again in Venice. Spaak's proposals, for a European Economic Community (EEC) and a European Atomic Energy Commission (Euratom), won support within the Six. By the Treaties of Rome, signed on 25 March 1957, the EEC and Euratom were established. In 1967 the ECSC, the EEC and Euratom were formally merged to form a single European Community.

The EEC, based on the structure of the ECSC, consisted of:

- A Council of Ministers.
- A Commission (like the ECSC's High Authority).
- A Court of Justice.
- A European Parliament (both shared with the ECSC).

The purpose of the EEC was primarily to bring together as far as possible the economic policies of all the member countries. This was seen as an essential step towards a united Europe.

By the Treaty of Paris, which established the ECSC, member governments pledged:

> *1 To substitute for historic rivalries a fusion of their essential interests.*
> *2 To establish, by creating an economic community, the foundation of a wider and deeper community, among peoples long divided by bloody conflicts.*
> *3 To lay the bases of institutions capable of giving direction to their future common destiny.*[7]

The EEC was formed:

> *1 In order to maintain Europe's place in the world.*
> *2 To restore her influence and prestige.*
> *3 To ensure a continuous rise in the living standards of her people.*[8]

This European Commission cartoon shows how some saw Europe after the Second World War.

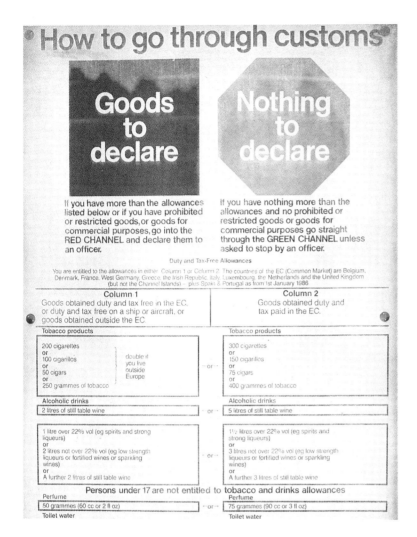

How to go through customs

Goods to declare

Nothing to declare

If you have more than the allowances listed below or if you have prohibited or restricted goods, or goods for commercial purposes, go into the RED CHANNEL and declare them to an officer.

If you have nothing more than the allowances and no prohibited or restricted goods or goods for commercial purposes go straight through the GREEN CHANNEL unless asked to stop by an officer.

Duty and Tax-Free Allowances

You are entitled to the allowances in either Column 1 or Column 2. The countries of the EC (Common Market) are Belgium, Denmark, France, West Germany, Greece, the Irish Republic, Italy, Luxembourg, the Netherlands and the United Kingdom (but not the Channel Islands) – plus Spain & Portugal as from 1st January 1986

Column 1	Column 2
Goods obtained duty and tax free in the EC, or duty and tax free on a ship or aircraft, or goods obtained outside the EC.	Goods obtained duty and tax paid in the EC.

Tobacco products		Tobacco products
200 cigarettes or 100 cigarillos or 50 cigars or 250 grammes of tobacco — double if you live outside Europe	— or —	300 cigarettes or 150 cigarillos or 75 cigars or 400 grammes of tobacco

Alcoholic drinks		Alcoholic drinks
2 litres of still table wine	— or —	5 litres of still table wine
1 litre over 22% vol (eg spirits and strong liqueurs) or 2 litres not over 22% vol (eg low strength liqueurs or fortified wines or sparkling wines) or A further 2 litres of still table wine	— or —	1½ litres over 22% vol (eg spirits and strong liqueurs) or 3 litres not over 22% vol (eg low strength liqueurs or fortified wines or sparkling wines) or A further 3 litres of still table wine

Persons under 17 are not entitled to tobacco and drinks allowances

Perfume		Perfume
50 grammes (60 cc or 2 fl oz)	— or —	75 grammes (90 cc or 3 fl oz)
Toilet water		Toilet water

The EEC is often known as the Common Market. Its essential aim is to get rid of all customs posts, such as the one in this picture, between member states. It is hoped this will come about in 1992, when there will be free trade within the EC.

As you read these two sets of points carefully, can you see that they contain two different concepts? Behind the foundation of the ECSC was the need for European unity to prevent further war. Following the collapse of the EDC, however, the EEC was more modest in its aims. It is primarily an economic organization. Consider the statistics below:

What do these statistics suggest to you of the EEC's economic power in relation to the rest of the world? Together the countries of the Community could successfully challenge the world's other great economic powers. But, in the long run, will greater economic co-operation automatically lead to closer political union?

Population (in millions) 1985		Total of world's exports		Total of world's imports	
EEC	322.6	EEC	19.8%	USA	22.5%
USSR	278.6	USA	14.6%	EEC	20.2%
USA	239.3	Japan	12.2%	Japan	8.5%
Japan	120.8	USSR	6.0%	USSR	5.4%
		Rest of world	47.4%	Rest of world	43.4%

4
EXPANSION OF THE COMMUNITY
New members

S INCE ITS FOUNDATION membership of the European Community has doubled. Despite the encouragement of Winston Churchill, the UK declined to become one of the original members. Instead, with Austria, Denmark, Norway, Portugal, Sweden and Switzerland, it formed the European Free Trade Association (EFTA) on 3 May 1960. EFTA was established to promote trade among its members, without the closer economic agreements which went with the EEC.

In the end, however, the UK did become a member of the Community. The following table tells the story of the Community's expanding membership:

Date	Events
1961	Ireland, Denmark and UK applied for membership. Preliminary negotiations held with Greece.
1962	Norway applied for membership. Preliminary negotiations held with Spain and Portugal.
1963	President de Gaulle of France, fearing that British membership of the Community would reduce French influence, vetoed UK's entry. Negotiations with Denmark, Ireland and Norway suspended.
1967	*Coup d'etat* in Greece set back its negotiations. UK, Ireland, Denmark and Norway re-applied for membership, but, as before, de Gaulle vetoed UK's application and negotiations with the other nations were suspended. The single European Community was created by merging the EEC, ECSC and Euratom.
1969	President de Gaulle resigned.
1970	UK, Ireland, Denmark and Norway again applied for membership.
1972	UK, Ireland and Denmark signed treaties to become members in 1973. As a result of a referendum Norway rejected membership.
1974	Britain's Labour government re-negotiated the terms of UK's membership.
1975	UK's re-negotiated terms accepted by the British people in a referendum. Greece applied for membership.
1977	Spain and Portugal applied for membership.
1979	Greece signed a treaty to become a member in 1981.
1985	Spain and Portugal signed treaties to become members of the Community in 1986.

◀ President Charles de Gaulle consistently blocked the UK's entry to the EC because he feared that, if the UK joined, French influence would be reduced and that of the USA would increase.

Irish politicians signing their country's entry to the EC in January 1972. The UK and Denmark signed at the same time, but membership did not come into effect until the following year.

Once a country is a member of the Community it has the following obligations:

- To abide by the Community's laws, treaties and policies.
- To send a minister to the Council of Ministers, a judge to the Court of Justice, and a representative (or two from the larger states) to the Commission.
- To carry out elections for the European Parliament.
- To contribute to the Community budget.
- To be prepared to work for the good of the Community as a whole, not just for national interests.

Why do countries join?

What is the cartoonist suggesting about the state of the UK compared with the rest of Europe? Do you think the artist is in favour of the UK's entry to the EC?

The reasons why countries join the European Community can be placed under two headings, practical and ideological. The practical reasons are the material benefits that membership brings to a country. The ideological reasons include the idea that a united Europe is of more benefit to European people, as well as the world at large, than a continent made up of small, separate countries.

In 1971 the Bishop of London argued in the House of Lords that the UK should join the European Community:

> *Entry to the Market must be in the end something of a matter of faith... disunity... has to be replaced by something based on common ideals, something still to be worked out and put into practice, so that Britain can work with other nations for a new and better Europe.*[9]

Edward Heath, the Conservative Prime Minister, arguing the case for the UK's entry into the EC in 1971.

Do you think that the Bishop was supporting the UK's entry for practical or ideological reasons?

The practical reasons for joining the Community are fourfold:

1   Access to a wider market for a country's manufactured goods and agricultural produce.
2   Wider job opportunities for a member country's citizens.
3   Community grants, which are paid to a country to help with specific projects or to rebuild depressed areas.
4   As a member of a large, powerful Community, a country can exercise more influence in the world. Together the states of Europe could be rated with the mighty USA and USSR.

When in 1971 the Lord Chancellor spoke of the UK's entry as a chance for 'greatness renewed' rather than 'the certainty of frustration and decline', under which of the four reasons would you list his argument?[10]

There are two ideological reasons for joining the Community. First, the formation of a European Community lessens considerably the chance of further European war. And second, a united Europe can help the poorer countries of the world much more effectively than any single country. Can you find both these arguments in the following speech by Prime Minister Edward Heath?

I have worked for a Europe which is going to play an increasing part in meeting the needs of those parts of the world which still lie in the shadow of want. I want Britain as a member of a Europe which ... will enjoy lasting peace and the greatest security.[11]

Why is membership opposed?

The idea of a European Community is not supported by everyone. Norway voted not to join, and the UK's entry was strongly opposed by people from both the Conservative and Labour Parties. Several European countries, for example Sweden, are unwilling to apply for membership.

The basic principle behind opposition to the Community is that membership involves a loss of national sovereignty. The Labour MP Barbara Castle – now a member of the European Parliament – said:

> …the government knew when they talked about monetary and economic union they were talking about the transfer of the central control of the House of Commons over taxation to the Brussels Community. They would have taxation without representation…[12]

When the UK was applying to join the Community, MPs with a strong sense of tradition and history argued that the move would undermine all that was distinctively British. A unique culture and political heritage would be destroyed. An example of this worry occurred when the Commission tried

A 1961 cartoon showing how hard the British found it to trust their wartime foes, the Germans.

KRUPP WORKS
THE OLD FIRM YOU CAN TRUST

SLAVE LABOUR

KRUPP: NEW EXTENSION

"I STRETCH OUT MY HAND TO WELCOME THE BRITISH INTO OUR COMMON MARKET AND SHOW THAT I'VE FORGIVEN THEM…."

Karen Cooper throws a bag of ink at Edward Heath as he arrives to sign the UK into the EC, 1972. What fears lay behind such protests?

to see that throughout the Community beer was sold in standard-sized glasses. This was opposed in the UK, and eventually abandoned, because it would have meant the end of the traditional British pint.

Opponents of the EC also often claimed that the UK's political and economic future lay with the Commonwealth. After the Second World War the UK granted independence to its former colonies. These now joined with the states that had gained independence earlier, such as Australia and New Zealand, to form the Commonwealth of Nations, with the Queen at its head. With member states from every corner of the globe, rich and poor, of many different racial and religious groupings, the Commonwealth is a truly world-wide organization. By joining the EC, many argued, the UK would be moving from a broader to a narrower outlook. It was also felt that the UK would be deserting trusted and long-standing trading partners, especially Australia and New Zealand.

British Labour MPs felt that the Community was a capitalist organization, opposed to socialism. Lord Shepherd feared that 'the main burden of entry would fall on the working class'.[13] What do you think he meant by this? Time and again the EC was termed a 'Rich Man's Club', not truly dedicated to the interests of the people, but to big business.

The Krupp armaments factory in Germany had been making weapons since the nineteenth century. What point do you think the artist is making in the cartoon opposite? Does he approve of the Common Market?

Countries that have decided to remain outside the Community do so for two reasons. First, they believe that they are economically better off alone. Norway, for example, has such plentiful oil supplies that it has no need of a Common Market. Second, these countries wish to be seen as politically neutral, not attached to a grouping that might take a strong, political stance. This view is widely held in neutral countries such as Sweden and Switzerland.

5
HOW THE COMMUNITY WORKS
The Council of Ministers

The Foreign Secretary, Sir Geoffrey Howe, who represents the UK's interests in the Council of Ministers. In the Council the clash between national and Community interest is often apparent.

T HE POLITICIANS WHO set up the EC thought that it would be like an oil rig, standing on four equal, strong legs. These were the Commission, the Council of Ministers, the Court of Justice and the European Parliament. In the late 1980s, however, the Council of Ministers was far more powerful than the other three institutions. The Council is the EC's decision-making body; nothing can happen in the Community

without the Council's approval.

The Council of Ministers has four levels:
1   The Committee of Permanent Representatives – COREPER. This committee consists of permanent representatives from the twelve member states. In consultation with the Parliament and the Commission, from whom it receives proposals, it is responsible for day-to-day decisions about which policies or new laws should be adopted by

the Community. All agreements have to be accepted later by the full Council of Ministers. For a policy to become law, it has to have the support of fifty-four votes. The voting power of individual members is based upon the size of their country's population: France, Germany, Italy and the UK have ten votes each; Spain has eight votes; Belgium, Greece, the Netherlands, and Portugal have five votes each; Denmark and Ireland have three votes; Luxembourg has two votes. However, if a country feels very strongly about an issue, it can sometimes use its veto. This stops the matter being accepted, even though there may be fifty-four votes in its favour.

2   Sectoral Councils. These meet, sometimes several times a week, to debate issues on which COREPER cannot agree. The relevant national ministers sit on the Councils. If, for example, there is disagreement over airline safety measures, the Community's transport ministers meet.

3   The Council of Ministers. This consists usually of the foreign ministers of the member states and meets about four times a year. The Council has to give formal approval to all decisions made at a lower level, as well as to review future Community policy.

4   The European Council – the Community 'Summit'. These often bitter meetings are held between the leaders of the twelve member states, each representing their own country's interests. Summits receive a great deal of media coverage, as when in Dublin (1979) and Luxembourg (1980) Margaret Thatcher negotiated ruthlessly for a reduction in the UK's contribution to the Community budget.

The first summit held after the accession of Spain and Portugal to the EC, 1986. What problems did Portugal bring to the EC?

The Commission

The European Commission lies at the heart of the Community. It is rather like a European civil service, except that it has many more functions. This makes it somewhat difficult for the British, accustomed to a non-political, impersonal civil service, to understand.

Essentially, the Commission performs five functions.

1 It is responsible for coming up with new ideas on the way the Community can be more harmoniously and efficiently run. For example, it produced the standard coding of food additives, 'E' numbers, which you can see in the nutritional information on the side of tins, packets and boxes.

2 It writes new Community laws and proposals for presentation to the European Parliament and Council of Ministers. European law comes in the form of Regulations, which apply to all states, or Decisions, which apply only to some states. Directives set targets, but leave it to the individual states to work out how they will achieve them. A Regulation or Decision might be on vehicle safety, a Directive concerned with the purity of drinking water.

3 It acts as a watchdog to ensure Community rules are being carried out. This quite often links with the Commission's fourth function.

4 It acts as a mediator when two or more Community states find that they cannot reach agreement over an issue, such as the quota of goods being traded between two countries.

5 It conducts diplomatic relations between the Community as a whole and other nations. In this capacity it is responsible for the Community's many commercial treaties.

Leon Brittan, once one of the leading figures in Margaret Thatcher's Cabinet, joined the Commission in 1989. He had to give up his seat in the House of Commons to do so.

The Commission is headed by seventeen commissioners (two each from the larger states, one from the smaller ones), one of whom is president, aided by four vice-presidents. A Commissioner, who has usually been a leading political figure in his own country, takes an oath to serve the Community as a whole. He or she is then responsible for a Directorate-General (DG), or area of the Commission's work. For example, DG6 is agriculture. Commissioners are

The Commission is very concerned about the pollution of beaches, not only for health reasons, but also because it affects the tourist industry.

aided by their personal 'cabinets', or staff.

The Commission has a huge task to perform, and it is very complicated. But you can get some idea of its efficiency when you realize that in 1985 its 10,037 employees were fewer than those employed by London's Wandsworth Borough Council.[14]

The European Parliament

The European Parliament is in many ways the most interesting of the Community's organizations. It is a symbol of the European commitment to democracy and co-operation. Moreover, it is constantly developing, trying to increase its power and influence over other branches of the administration.

There are 518 members of the European Parliament (MEPs) from all parts of the political spectrum, as the illustration opposite shows. Why do you think that only seven independents were elected in 1984? The map below shows how the number of MEPs allotted to each country is proportional to its population. Much of the detailed work of the Parliament is done in one of its eighteen permanent committees. These deal with such issues as the European Budget, Women's Rights, Regional Policy and Planning, and Overseas Development. As the Parliament itself points out:

From 1 January 1973 to 1 July 1982 over £866.4 million has been spent in the UK from the Regional Fund and over £732.5 million from the Social Fund. As examples of use, some 15–20% of spending by the British Manpower Services Commission is financed by the Social Fund and the Regional Fund has helped projects such as roads, bridges and industrial development...

A country's allocation of MEPs is roughly in proportion to its population. The map shows the division of the 1984–9 Parliament. Why are the largest countries all given 81 MEPs?

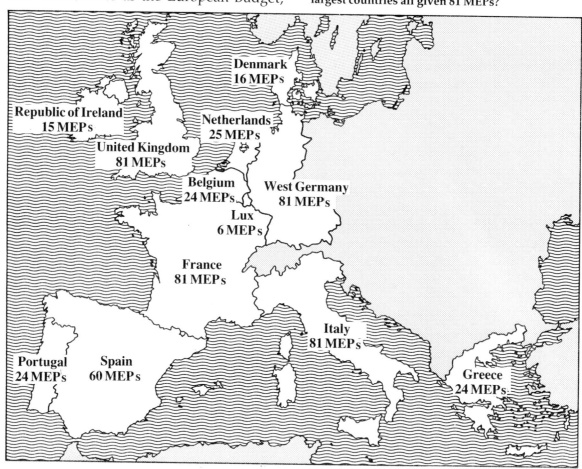

Denmark 16 MEPs

Republic of Ireland 15 MEPs

Netherlands 25 MEPs

United Kingdom 81 MEPs

Belgium 24 MEPs

West Germany 81 MEPs

Lux 6 MEPs

France 81 MEPs

Italy 81 MEPs

Portugal 24 MEPs

Spain 60 MEPs

Greece 24 MEPs

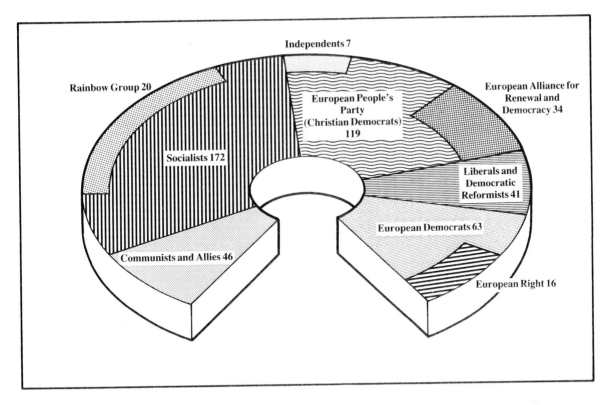

The size of these funds owes much to the pressure of the European Parliament.[15] There are nine official languages in the Community – those of all the member countries except Eire and Luxembourg – and all speeches in the Parliament are translated simultaneously so that all MEPs can understand the proceedings.

The Parliament itself meets in Strasbourg, the administration in Luxembourg, and the committees in Brussels. People complain of the cost of this split-site operation, but in fact in 1986 the Parliament cost the British people only one pence a week each.

MEPs are elected every five years from the member countries, which decide which electoral system to use. In 1984 only the UK used the traditional first-past-the-post method, all others preferring proportional representation. In the Community as a whole, turnout for the 1984 elections was over 60 per cent, but in the UK only 32 per cent voted – a sharp reminder of how isolationist the British still are.

A diagram showing all the different parties represented in the European Parliament, 1984–9. With so many groups do you think it is difficult for the Parliament to speak with a single voice?

The functions of the Parliament are to:
- Act as a watchdog on the Commission and the Council: it has the power to take the Council to a Court, and may ask for the Commission to be dismissed. It may also reject the Community's international agreements.
- Debate matters of Community interest.
- Propose and debate new Community laws. In some fields the Parliament has a virtual veto over the Council of Ministers' recommendations.
- Work with the Commission and the Council to produce the Community budget.

Why do you think that the Parliament is anxious to increase its powers in this last mentioned area?

The Community's Courts

Lord MacKenzie Stuart, who was President of the European Court for fifteen years. During this period the number of cases dealt with by the Court more than doubled.

There are four international courts in Europe. The International Court at the Hague, which has very little power, comes under the auspices of the United Nations. Citizens of countries that have signed the European Convention on Human Rights can appeal to the European Court of Human Rights if they feel that they have had their rights infringed. For example, in 1980 the Court, which meets in Strasbourg, ruled

that 'the laws under which Britain detains and questions people who may have information about terrorism' broke the Convention.[16] Although it involves the Community, the Court is not part of its organization.

There are two Community Courts, the Court of Auditors, which checks the Community accounts, and the European Court of Justice in Luxembourg. Its purpose is to rule on disputes involving Community legislation and the treaties that established the Community. Thirteen judges sit on the Court, at least one from each member state, with a president in overall charge. The president is now Mr Ole Due from Denmark, who replaced the Scottish judge Lord Mac-Kenzie Stuart, previously president for fifteen years. The Court handles over 350 cases a year, each one taking an average of twenty-one months. In 1988 a preliminary Court of First Instance was established in an effort to relieve the judges of some of their workload.

Cases can involve individuals, companies, or even governments themselves. At the end of 1988, for example, the Commission took the Spanish government to the Court for breaking the Community rules over the discharge of toxic waste into rivers. The Commission successfully claimed that the Spanish had allowed the River Gallego in Aragon to become polluted because EC guidelines were not being enforced.

The Italian government has been brought before the Court over a hundred times. Some issues are trivial, as when it was accused of over-taxing bananas. More serious was the time when it failed to obey European rules on toxic waste, trying to dump tonnes of it from the German ship, *Karin B*. Ultimately the Court cannot force a government to obey its rulings: there are thirty-six Court rulings that the Italians have yet to enforce. The Court has also ruled on matters as widespread as the powers of the European Parliament, and the tax obligations of the *Daily Mail*. What do you think Lord Stuart meant when he declared, 'Nationality ends at the Court's doorstep'?[17]

The *Karin B* carrying Italian toxic waste. The Italian government rushed through laws to comply with Community directives on the subject of toxic waste.

6
THE COMMUNITY AT WORK
Making policy

SINCE COMING TO POWER in 1979, Margaret Thatcher's Conservative government has changed numerous aspects of British life, from taxation policy to the school curriculum. Many of these radical policies were formulated before the prime minister took office. Once elected leader of the nation, she then devoted her time and energies to put them into practice. Nothing could be more different from the way the government of the European Community operates.

The key to Community decision-making

Jacques Delors, President of the European Commission, is one of the chief supporters of the Community's 'Project 1992'.

is compromise. Each new policy has to be acceptable to the governments of all twelve member states, as well as the major organs of Community government. Even then it can be overturned by the European Court if it rules that the decision contravenes the Treaties that established the Community. At every stage of the discussion pressure groups, trade unions, companies, local governments and other interested parties put their views as forcefully as they can.

New policy originates with the Commission, headed since 1981 by Jacques Delors. In the late 1980s it was much concerned with preparing the way for 1992, when the Community aims to become a single economic unit, without national tariffs or barriers of any kind. One step towards this has involved lengthy discussion with companies, governments and trade unions about government public-works contracts. A way had to be found to ensure that they were offered on equal terms to firms from all Community countries.

From the Commission a proposal passes to the Parliament, and to the Economic and

The EC spent a lot of time in 1988 reaching an agreement on small-car emission controls. The French are the main producers of such cars: why do you think they pressed for lower standards?

Social Committee. The latter is a consultative body of 189 members, made up of representatives from employers, workers and pressure groups. After these two groups have discussed a proposal, it is sent to the Council of Ministers. Once again it is discussed and often amended to fit national needs. An example of a Community policy decision is the agreement, finally reached in 1988, on new exhaust emission standards for small cars for 1992. The original proposals had to be relaxed to meet French requirements. New Regulations, Decisions and Directives then return to the Commission to be put into effect. Do you agree that the complicated decision-making process means that, 'What is clear about the future of the European Community is that it will develop and take shape according to the wishes of its people'?[18]

Social Policy

Women's Rights

The Treaties that established the European Community make only one reference to women's rights. Article 119 of the Treaty of Rome runs, 'Each member state shall ensure the application of the principle that men and women should receive equal pay for equal work'.[19] If the Treaty were being drawn up today, what other rights would you expect women to want protected?

Since 1976 a series of directives has been produced to promote the interests of women. In member countries there is supposed to be no discrimination between men and women in employment, training and conditions of work. There are also laws covering sickness, pensions, unemployment benefit, taxation and other matters. But it is up to individual countries to put these into effect: there has been a string of cases before the European Court in which women have complained at not being allowed equality with men in these areas. The Parliament, which has many women MEPs, has put constant pressure on the Commission and the Council to do more to help women. Do you think that it is significant that only in 1988 were the first two female Commissioners appointed?

Employment

In the 1970s and 1980s unemployment

Average income per head in the EC ranges from £7,725 to £3,175 (1987). The Regional Development Fund tries to redistribute wealth from the richer areas to poorer ones, such as southern Italy.

A British employment office. Unemployment was hardly a matter for discussion when the EC was formed but now it is a major problem. Why do you think it makes the Community policy of the free movement of labour from one country to another difficult to operate?

became a serious problem for the Community for the first time. The Commission produced an overall strategy to deal with it. This involved energy conservation, concentration on new industries, and speeding up the development of a single European market – the Community's aim for 1992. By that year it is hoped that all tariffs between EC countries will have gone, enabling goods to pass freely from one country to another without delay or additional cost. The war on unemployment also meant improving the Community's monetary system. In practical terms, to reduce the figure of 16.4 million unemployed in 1986 (37 per cent of whom were under the age of 25), the Community gave countries substantial grants through its Regional Development Fund, Employment Grant Schemes and other sources. Between 1975 and 1985 the UK received almost a quarter of the total of all the money given by the Regional Development Fund.

Other Community work in the field of employment has concentrated on improving conditions at work, helping the handicapped and protecting migrant workers. For example, in December 1988 the European Parliament debated health and safety at work and VDU screens. Ken Collins, the UK Euro MP for Strathclyde East, argued that it was important for the EC to legislate in this area, 'including a four hour limit on working with a computer or word processor screen on account of eye strain or other threats to health.'[20] The proposal was approved. From this it can be seen that there is hardly a corner of the lives of Europeans that is not now affected by the Community.

Other Policies

Although it is not a high Community priority, there have been schemes to help the disadvantaged. A Poverty Action Programme, for example, ran from 1985–8 at a cost of £15.4 million. At present the Community is looking seriously into ways of dealing with the rapidly growing problem of drug abuse.

Trade and industry

The highly successful Ariane rocket, demonstrating how effective European technology can be when individual nations pool their resources.

As we have seen, 'the essential aim of the founders of the European Community was to bring the member countries closer together, first by economic co-operation and integration, leading gradually to greater political co-operation'.[21] In other words, a 'Common Market' would lead to a 'European Community'. How did this differ from other plans for a united Europe?

The present aim of the Community is for it to be a single market by 1992. This means that all goods can be sold on equal terms in any member state. To this end the Commission has produced many laws freeing competition within the Community. But the scheme has serious political overtones.

The price of an article is made up of four elements. First, the cost of the raw materials. Second, the cost of labour, packaging and marketing. Third, profit for the producer and retailer, and fourth, tax. For a single market, the last item (tax) has to be uniform throughout all states. In order to achieve this, member state governments have to surrender their right to tax their people as they wish. This would apply to Value Added Tax (VAT) and other sales taxes, as well as customs duties. For example, from 1992 passengers will no longer benefit from 'duty free' goods on ferry and plane trips to Europe. This would obviously force up the cost of such journeys.

However, using its enormous economic power, the Community has managed to negotiate numerous economic treaties with countries all over the world. The first of these was with African countries; since then many others have followed; for example, an agreement with Hungary in 1988 to remove all quotas on Hungarian imports into the Community by 1995.

Community industrial policy is based around two themes: helping older, declining industries such as coal, steel and textiles, and encouraging new industries. In this second field, frightened by the fact that in 1984, for example, nine out of ten video recorders used in the Community were made in Japan, the Community invested millions of pounds in basic research, as well as in specific industries such as electronics, biotechnology and telecommunications.

By 1992 all tariffs between EC states should have been abolished. This will cut the profits of duty-free shops and increase the cost of travel.

Energy and the environment

In the long term, energy and environmental policies are the most important that the Community follows. They are closely related. It is now widely recognized that we are using up our sources of conventional energy at an alarming rate, while at the same time polluting the planet and destroying the environment. As a group of some of the most scientifically advanced nations, the Community feels a responsibility to the rest of the world, as well as to itself, to face these problems directly.

Consider these statistics:

- The Community is the world's largest oil importer.
- Over 30 per cent of the Community energy is used for heating, lighting, hot water and ventilation.
- 25 per cent of the Community's energy is used for transport.

In the light of these figures, it is easy to see why the Community's energy policy has two sides to it:

1 Reducing dependence on oil, by encouraging changes to other forms of heating (such as electricity), and funding research into alternative energy sources, such as nuclear energy and tidal power.

2 Conserving energy through policies such as more efficient insulation, and encouraging the use of public transport.

A single Community environmental policy began with the European Summit meeting in Paris in 1972. The programme sought to reduce and, if at all possible, to remove all

Community law now makes it much more difficult for areas of environmental beauty or interest to be despoiled.

Community funds have been used for research into safe nuclear power, without much success.

environmental pollution; to protect the earth's atmosphere; to ensure that the conditions for a healthy life (such as clean water and space) were available to all; to preserve the natural environment; and to work with all other nations to achieve these aims.

Almost one hundred laws have been issued to put these policies into effect. Matters covered range from banning certain dangerous weed-killers to making it compulsory to inform the public before starting any scheme that might cause damage to the environment.

Yet environmental issues are tricky. The use of fluorocarbons in aerosol sprays is a case in point. When released into the atmosphere they destroy the protective ozone layer around the planet, leading to serious environmental consequences. But reprocessing fluorocarbons is expensive, and alternative aerosol propellants are costly. Who will meet the cost of creating a less polluted environment?

The budget

Each member country of the EC has its own money, or currency. These currencies can be exchanged freely; for example, you can go to a bank and change an English pound for about 10.5 French francs. But the rate of exchange is continually changing. This can make Community funding extremely difficult to organize: when a country receives money from the Regional Development Fund, what currency should it be paid in, and at what rate of exchange?

The answer was to create a single European Currency Unit (ECU) in 1979. The ECU's rate of exchange with members' currencies is allowed to fluctuate only within narrow margins, and the idea has proved a considerable success. To the disappointment of many, the UK has failed to join this European Monetary System (EMS). Although several members of her government are in favour of the idea, Prime Minister Thatcher has kept the UK out of EMS, because she:

> *probably fears that conceding it would intensify pressure to go for full monetary integration, with unacceptable consequences for British sovereignty.*[22]

Are Thatcher's worries about the EMS economic or political?

Each year the Community raises a budget from all the member countries. In 1989 it was 44,000,837.6 ECU, coming mainly from Community customs, agricultural levies and a proportion of each member's VAT receipts. For ten years after joining the EC the UK complained that its contributions to the budget were too high, and it was not until the Summit of June 1984 that the problem was solved.

The bulk of the Community budget is spent on agriculture and fisheries policies. The remainder goes towards research,

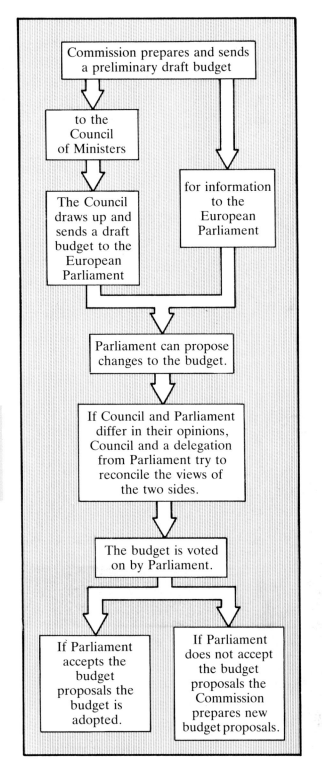

{

}

▼The bulk of the Community's budget is spent on supporting agriculture, at times leading to embarrassing surpluses of foodstuffs, as this 'butter mountain' shows.

▲Margaret Thatcher often complained that the UK's contribution to the EC budget was too high. Her inflexible attitude did not endear her to European politicians, but in the end she had her way.

energy and transport, social policy, regional development, administration, overseas aid and refunds to member states.

Who controls the budget? The diagram opposite explains how it is drawn up. Why do you think that the financial magazine, *The Economist* described this procedure as 'an awkward exercise in power sharing?'[23] What does it mean by 'power sharing'?

Control over the budget is one of the most important powers of the European Parliament. The Community is made up of democratic states, so it is essential that an elected assembly should have the final say over how the people's money is spent.

The Community is also trying to harmonize excise taxes and VAT by 1992, but there is little chance of this coming about in time. The road to a united Europe is not a smooth one, but, as the politicians need to keep reminding themselves, there is no real alternative.

Education and culture

The European Community is a bewildering pattern of diversity and uniformity. Its surface area of 2.26 million square kilometres is only about a quarter that of the USA, while its population is only about 7 per cent of the world total. Yet this comparatively small, densely populated group of states includes an enormous range of cultures and organizations.

There are nine official languages (while there is only one official language in the USA, the USSR and Japan), and hundreds of complex dialects. Compared with the relatively uniform diet of most Americans, the eating habits of the Europeans range from the pasta and wine of the hot south, to Scottish porridge and whisky. European nations eat, sleep and work at different times of the day. Their views on family life are not the same, nor are their manners or personal priorities.

However, to an outsider, people from the Community's nations appear remarkably similar. Americans, for example, are starting to refer to people from France, Germany or Greece, not as members of a particular country, but as Europeans. Soon we will be carrying European passports in place of our national ones. Already the Community is learning to speak with a single voice in world politics: in April 1982 it agreed to ban the import of all Argentinian products, in support of the UK's action to regain the Falkland Islands. In 1988 it welcomed, as one nation, the rejection of violence by the Palestine Liberation Organization.

Wolfgang Amadeus Mozart (1756–91), the brilliant Austrian composer, whose music forms an important part of a single European cultural heritage.

Diversity within unity is one of the themes of the EC, which has to be very careful not to interfere with treasured local customs and traditions, such as the *Fête des Marins* at Honfleur, France.

Europeans of the Community have much common history. They were nearly all at one time under Roman rule. Painters, scholars, musicians and poets have moved freely between states, their work and talent receiving international recognition. The Christian heritage, too, has served to provide a common cultural foundation.

Therefore, the Community has not felt it wise to pass laws to bring countries together in terms of culture or education. There is already sufficient unity, which economic and political co-operation will foster. The only major step, apart from agreeing common rights in areas such as employment and mutual recognition of professional qualifications, has been in language teaching. It is now compulsory for school children of all member states to learn at least one other European language.

Agriculture and fishing

The Common Agricultural Policy (CAP) is one of the most controversial aspects of the European Community. A careful look at these figures will help you to work out why:

- Community workers in agriculture: 10.7 million.
- Community workers in manufacturing industry: 41.2 million.
- Agriculture produces 3.3 per cent of the Community wealth.
- Manufacturing industry produces 38.4 per cent of the Community wealth.
- Over half the Community budget is spent on CAP.[24]

In other words, the Community spends a good deal of its money helping a relatively small industry. Which of these can you live without: shoes, food, cars, or televisions? Agriculture is the essential industry. That is why the Community gives it a high priority.

However, the situation is not that simple.

Why do you think the Community needed to reach an agreed Common Fisheries Policy?

Large farms are more efficient than small farms. 81.9 per cent of British farms are larger than 50 hectares, while in Greece the figure is 3.1 per cent. Agriculture provides 18.5 per cent of the Greek national income, but only 1.7 per cent in the UK.[25] Do you think it is fair that the British complain that their efficient large farms are subsidizing Greek inefficiency, when agriculture is so important to the Greek economy?

A further problem is that of over-production, or surpluses. The media like to refer to these as 'wine lakes' or 'food mountains'. In 1987 the Community held these surpluses (in 1,000s tonnes):

Butter	1,006
Wheat	6,897
Olive oil	287[26]

Why does the Community spend so much on agriculture, when it is merely over-producing food? The answer lies in the first two aims of the CAP:

- To increase agricultural productivity.
- To guarantee farm prices and to see that farmers have a fair standard of living.
- To stabilize markets.
- To ensure reasonable consumer prices.
- To ensure the free movement of agricultural goods.[27]

The Community is torn, therefore, between helping farmers, particularly in the poorer areas, and encouraging efficiency. Agreement has already been reached on a Common Fisheries Policy, which strikes a balance between helping the fishing industry and conserving stocks in the sea. Gradually the situation in agriculture is also coming under control. The surpluses above, for example, were reduced in 1988, but progress is very slow.

► A combine harvester at work on a large farm in the UK.

◄ Harvesting by hand in southern France. One of the Community's most trying problems is balancing the needs of large, efficient farms and small, less modernized ones.

7
EUROPE AND THE WORLD
Defence of the West

T HE EUROPEAN COMMUNITY is not a military alliance. Nevertheless, one of its stated aims is the 'preservation and strengthening of peace and liberty'.[28]

After the Second World War Europe divided between the Soviet-dominated East and the capitalist countries of the West, who looked to the USA for support and leadership. Between the two sides there descended what Winston Churchill termed an 'iron curtain'. During the late 1940s, and throughout the 1950s and 1960s, there was frightening tension between East and West, known as the Cold War, which at times looked as if it might break out into 'hot' or open war. The map below shows on which side the countries ranged themselves.

The Western nations formed the North Atlantic Treaty Organization (NATO) in 1949. West Germany joined this alliance in 1954, and soon afterwards the Eastern bloc

The division of Europe after the Second World War.

44

◄The history and culture of Turkey is vastly different to that of other EC nations. That is one reason why politicians are hesitant to welcome Turkey into Europe.

▼Checkpoint Charlie, between the British and Soviet sectors of Berlin. Despite the recent improvement in relations between East and West, Berlin, an isolated enclave of the EC, remains a potential source of serious tension.

signed their own military alliance, known as the Warsaw Pact. Before the Warsaw Pact the nations under Soviet domination had created the Council for Mutual Economic Aid (Comecon) in 1949, to facilitate economic co-operation. To some extent the ECSC, Euratom and EEC, which became the European Community in 1967, were Western Europe's response to Comecon. By co-operating to increase the wealth of the West, the Community is strengthening its defences against the East.

Since the late 1980s there has been much discussion over whether Turkey should join the Community. As you can see from the map, from a defence point of view it is essential for the West that Turkey does not come under Communist influence. Yet Turkey is relatively poor, with a bad record on human rights, a different history and cultural traditions to other EC nations. Do you think it should be allowed to join the Community?

Since the foundation of the Community, East-West relations have changed. In June 1987 the Community and Comecon formally recognized each other for the first time; since then there have been trade agreements between the Community and individual Comecon countries, such as Hungary.

Trading partners

The European Community is the world's largest trading bloc. It handles over one-fifth of all the world's exports, exporting and importing a quarter of its Gross Domestic Product (GDP) (the wealth produced by its manufacturers and services). Behind these impressive statistics, however, there are problems:

- Irish imports value 64 per cent of her GDP, while her exports are only 47 per cent. The figures for Germany are 24 per cent and 26 per cent.
- 61 per cent of Belgium and Luxembourg's imports come from Community countries, but only 42 per cent of Italy's imports come from this source.[29]

What difficulties do you think the Commission has to face when trying to supervise the Community's trading arrangements? Three problems suggested in the figures above are:

1 Some countries import far more than they export, thus leaving themselves always short of foreign currency.

2 Imports and exports play a far greater part in the economies of some countries than they do in others.

Southampton docks, UK. More world trade is handled by the EC than any other trading group or nation. Community trade policy has been described as 'Neither fortress nor sieve.' What does this mean?

British pig farmers deliver a petition (and a pig!) to 10 Downing Street as a protest at what they feel to be discrimination against their produce in the EEC.

3 Some member states trade mostly with other Community countries, while others have more trade with the rest of the world.

The Commission, therefore, seeks to do three things. First, it aims to make all trade within the Community as free of taxes or duties as possible. This is dealt with on pages 34–5. Second, the Community, which is not self-sufficient in many vital commodities, such as oil, tin, lead and bauxite (from which aluminium is made), has to remain flexible and competitive. Third, as well as securing trade agreements with nations outside the EC, it negotiates, not always successfully, to ensure that foreign imports do not destroy the Community's own industries.

In 1988-9 there were disagreements with Japan and the USA, the Community's largest rivals. The first concerned Japanese Nissan cars, largely manufactured and assembled in the UK. The trouble with the USA arose over the Community's claim that beef exported from the USA contained too many dangerous growth hormones.

The developing world

Pictures of the Ethiopian famine victims bring home the uncomfortable difference between the standard of living in EC countries and the developing world. Through the Lomé Convention the Community helps over sixty developing nations.

From its very beginning the European Community recognized that the need to work closely with the world's poorer nations, the so-called Third World, was essential. The reasons for this are moral, political and economic.

It is clearly morally wrong for the inhabitants of a wealthy Europe, who are about $5,000 a year better off now than they were twenty years ago, to ignore the fact that 750 million people in the world live in abject poverty.[30] If we have any conscience, we must try to do something about this.

The huge differences in living standards between the developed and developing nations breed jealousy and aggression. A prosperous nation is often contented, while the poor have nothing to lose by resorting to violence. For the future peace of the world, therefore, the rich must try to spread their wealth more equally over the world.

Finally, the developing nations take 40 per cent of the Community's exports, and from them the Community receives all but 10 per cent of its raw materials.[31] The wealthier the nations of the world become, the more they will be able to trade with the Community, buying its sophisticated exports, such as cars and aeroplanes. So, from an economic point of view, it is to the Community's advantage to build up the economies of Third World nations.

What is the Community doing?

1 The EC and its member countries give more financial aid to developing countries than the USA, USSR and Japan combined.
2 The Yaoundé and Lomé Conventions (1963 and 1975, renewed) help the countries that have signed them (Africa, the Caribbean and Pacific – called ACP nations) in four ways. 99.5 per cent of their exports to the Community enter duty-free. A special system, known as STABEX, guarantees stable earnings for ACP countries' exports to the EC. By the MINEX system, ACP countries receive special help with crucial exports such as bauxite. Billions of ECUs are available, through the Community and the European Investment Bank, for ACP projects.

Some observers claim that EC aid is primarily given to develop industries, such as mining, which benefit Europe as much as the poorer country receiving the aid. Why, therefore, can EC aid be seen as simply conscience money?

Slums of Bombay. What can be done to prevent the gap between rich and poor nations widening?

Into the future

By the mid 1980s the politicians of the Community were worried about the way the EC was developing. You can see the reasons for this in the words of Lord Cockfield, the British Vice-President of the Commission:

Great progress was made in the early years. But with the recessions of the 1970s that progress slowed down and was halted. But our competitors – particularly the United States of America and Japan and the emerging industrial economies of the Far East – continued to forge ahead. In contrast with our competitors our record on productivity, on innovation and on employment has not been good. We have at the last count 16.8 million of our people unemployed. We cannot continue that way.[32]

Although the number of countries in the Community had doubled, it was still a very long way from being a 'Common Market'. Therefore, in June 1985 the Commission produced a White Paper (discussion document) outlining proposals to create a fully unified internal market by 1992. There will then be a 'Europe without frontiers'. By the end of 1988 most of the plans were ready. To help progress a Single European Act came into force in 1987. This amended the Treaty of Rome for the first time, rendering decision-making easier. More decisions

Construction of the Channel Tunnel. The Tunnel is an important symbol of British willingness to be seen as European, rather than as a westward-looking island.

Lord Cockfield, an outstanding British Vice-President of the European Commission, who worked tirelessly to convince his fellow Europeans that the UK was fully committed to the principles of the EC.

could be taken with the majority support of member countries rather than having to reach unanimous agreement. And more influence was given to the people of Europe through their elected European Parliament. The road to a united Europe was now much more clearly visible.

Nevertheless, many obstacles remained. Some of these were matters of detail. For example, Spain complained that progress to 1992 would cost Spain 800,000 jobs.[33] Some national leaders, led by Margaret Thatcher, were worried about their governments' loss of power over the nations they were elected to govern: a 'loss of sovereignty'. Margaret Thatcher herself also warned:

> Just when countries such as the Soviet Union are learning that success depends on dispersing power, some in the [EC] want to move in the opposite direction.[34]

But is there a real alternative? Can you imagine the consequences for Europe and the whole world if the European Community were to collapse?

The members of the Community

Belgium

Size:	31,000 sq km
Population:	9.9 million
MEPs:	24
GNP per capita:	$8,126
Major industries:	Coal, industrial manufacture
Date of joining EC:	1957
Currency:	Belgian franc
Languages:	French, Flemish

Housing the Commission in its capital city, Brussels, Belgium is at the very heart of the Community. Highly dependent on foreign trade, with excellent communications to most other EC countries, and with strong cosmopolitan traditions, the country epitomizes the spirit of the Community.

Denmark

Size:	43,000 sq km
Population:	5.1 million
MEPs:	16
GNP per capita:	$11,020
Major industries:	Industrial manufacture, agriculture
Date of joining EC:	1974
Currency:	Krone
Language:	Danish

The most northerly of the continental Community members, the kingdom of Denmark joined the EC in 1974, bringing with it long traditions of a tolerant and rich civilization. It is the wealthiest of the Community states.

Members of the European Community.

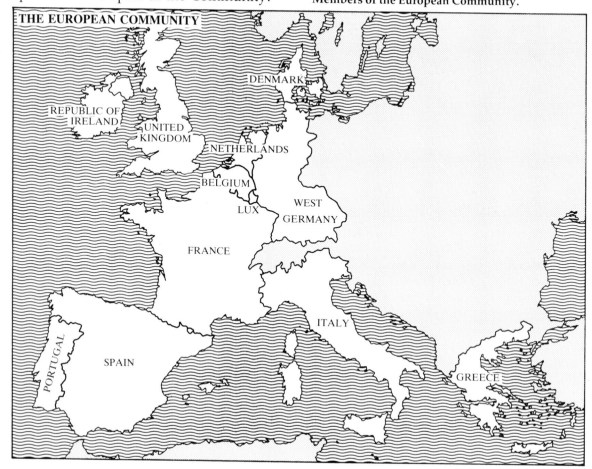

THE EUROPEAN COMMUNITY

A French girl in traditional national costume.

Federal Republic of Germany

Size: 249,000 sq km
Population: 61.4 million
MEPs: 81
GNP per capita: $10,633
Major industries: Industrial manufacture
Date of joining EC: 1957
Currency: Deutschmark
Language: German

After the formation of the German Empire in 1871, the spectre of aggressive German power haunted Europe. Now, after two world wars, and with the nation divided between the Federal Republic and the Communist Democratic Republic, West Germany is not only economically the most powerful Community member, but also one of the most committed to the cause of European peace and unity.

France

Size: 544,000 sq km
Population: 55.2 million
MEPs: 81
GNP per capita: $9,358
Major industries: Industrial manufacture, tourism, agriculture
Date of joining EC: 1957
Currency: French franc
Language: French

For centuries before 1871 French power had dominated the continent of Europe, and for many years President de Gaulle vetoed further expansion of the Community's original six members, fearing further diminution of French influence. Now, despite a fervent defence of national interests on occasion, France is one of the Community's leading powers, providing many of the politicians who have been most forceful in calling for a united Europe.

Greece

Size: 132,000 sq km
Population: 9.9 million
MEPs: 24
GNP per capita: $3,505
Major industries: Tourism, agriculture, shipping
Date of joining EC: 1981
Currency: Drachma
Language: Greek

Greece is the most agricultural of EC member states, and also one of the least densely populated. Under military rule between 1967 and 1974, the country now looks to the Community to help it develop its economy and secure democracy. Greece won its independence from the Turkish Empire in the early nineteenth century. There is still hostility between Greece and Turkey, complicating negotiations over Turkey's wish to join the EC.

Greek peasant in working dress.

Ireland

Size: 70,000 sq km
Population: 3.5 million
MEPs: 15
GNP per capita: $5,120
Major industries: Agriculture, tourism
Date of joining EC: 1974
Currency: Irish pound
Languages: English, Irish

Ireland is divided between the North, which is part of the UK, and the Republic of Eire in the south. The Republic is the least densely populated of the Community member states. It receives large sums from the Community Regional Development Fund, but still finds it difficult to attract overseas investment and prevent talented Irish individuals from seeking employment abroad.

Italy

Size: 301,000 sq km
Population: 57.1 million
MEPs: 81
GNP per capita: $6,208
Major industries: Industrial manufacture, tourism, agriculture
Date of joining EC: 1957
Currency: Lira
Language: Italian

Sharply divided between the prosperous north and the poorer south, in some ways Italy is the maverick of the Community. It does not have traditions of strong central government and Community law is not easily enforced. Yet there is little doubt about Italian belief in eventual European unity.

Luxembourg

Size: 3,000 sq km
Population: 0.4 million
MEPs: 6
GNP per capita: $8,721
Major industries: Iron and steel, agriculture
Date of joining EC: 1957
Currency: Luxembourg franc
Languages: German, French

The Grand Duchy of Luxembourg was established as an independent state in 1815. It is an original member of the Community, houses many European organizations, such as the European Court of Justice, and is one of the most enthusiastic supporters of the idea of European unity. Because it is by far the smallest of the EC member states, its economy is totally dependent on EC membership.

The Netherlands

Size: 41,000 sq km
Population: 14.5 million
MEPs: 25
GNP per capita: $9,190
Major industries: Industrial manufacture, agriculture, petrochemicals
Date of joining EC: 1957
Currency: Guilder
Language: Dutch

Dutch girls at a Gouda cheese market.

A small, industrial trading nation such as the Netherlands, vulnerable to foreign invasion, is ideally suited to the concept of a United Europe. It was one of the original members and, particularly through the development of magnificent ports, has benefited considerably from Community membership.

Portugal

Size:	92,000 sq km
Population:	10.2 million
MEPs:	24
GNP per capita:	$2,055
Major industries:	Agriculture, tourism, textiles
Date of joining EC:	1986
Currency:	Escudo
Language:	Portuguese

Until recently Portugal controlled an extensive overseas empire. Since the Second World War this poorest of the Community's states has been undergoing a period of readjustment, the climax of which was being accepted into the Community with Spain in 1986. Membership can only help the relatively weak economy, although communications with other EC states are difficult.

Spain

Size:	505,000 sq km
Population:	38.6 million
MEPs:	60
GNP per capita:	$4,237
Major industries:	Tourism, agriculture, industrial manufacture
Date of joining EC:	1986
Currency:	Peseta
Languages:	Spanish, Catalan

Spain's recent history is dominated by bitter civil war (1936–9) and the subsequent fascist dictatorship of General Franco, which ended only in 1975. Since then this relatively underdeveloped nation, still stressed by internal separatist movements, has welcomed democracy and membership of the EC with both enthusiasm and relief.

United Kingdom

Size:	244,000 sq km
Population:	56.6 million
MEPs:	81
GNP per capita:	$8,072
Major industries:	Industrial manufacture, tourism, financial services
Date of joining EC:	1974
Currency:	Pound Sterling
Languages:	English, Welsh, Gaelic

Until recently in control of a world-wide empire, and still in close alliance with the Commonwealth, the United Kingdom can be seen as the most reluctant Community member. Its budget contributions and fears over loss of national sovereignty in 1992 have often caused more committed Europeans to despair. Yet the UK has brought to the Community years of democratic and parliamentary experience as well as considerable skill in international diplomacy.

Important dates

Date	Events
c.410	Collapse of the Roman Empire in the West.
800	Charlemagne crowned Holy Roman Emperor.
c.1309	Dante's *The Monarchia,* urging European unity.
c.1324	Marsiglio of Padua's *Defensor Pacis,* defending the idea of a united, secular government for Christendom.
1638	The French Duke of Sully's *Memoirs,* calling for a politically united Europe.
1807	Napoleon Bonaparte in control of virtually all continental Europe.
1815	Following the collapse of the Napoleonic Empire, the major states of Europe sought to establish lasting peace at the Congress of Vienna.
1861	Emergence of the Italian state.
1871	Germany united into a single empire.
1914-18	The First World War.
1919	League of Nations established in the Treaty of Versailles.
1923	Count Coudenhove-Kalergi's *Paneuropa,* suggesting common economic policies for European states.
1933	Adolf Hitler comes to power in Germany.
1935	Italian dictator Mussolini ignores the League of Nations and invades Abyssinia.
1939–45	Second World War.
1946	Winston Churchill calls for a 'United States of Europe'.
1948-9	Russian blockade of West Berlin, which was kept supplied by Allied aircraft.
1948–52	American aid, as part of the Marshall Plan, administered by the Organization for European Economic Co-operation (OEEC).
1949	Council of Europe established. Establishment of Comecon (Council for Mutual Economic Assistance).
1950	North Atlantic Treaty Organization (NATO) formed. The Schuman Plan calls for the European Coal and Steel Community (ECSC), and a possible Federation of Europe.
1951	ECSC established with six members.
1952–4	Failure of plans for a European Defence Community and European Political Community.
1954	Warsaw Pact set up.
1955	At the Messina Conference the Six prepare for greater economic co-operation.
1956	Venice Conference, laying the foundations for the European Economic Community (EEC) and European Atomic Energy Commission (Euratom).
1957	Treaties of Rome establish the EEC and Euratom. European Free Trade Association (EFTA) set up.
1962	Beginning of the Common Agricultural Policy (CAP).
1963	Failure of negotiations for Britain, Denmark, Ireland and Norway to join the Community. The Yaoundé Convention, linking the Community to many developing African nations.
1967	British, Danish, Irish and Norwegian efforts to join the Community again rejected. The EEC, ECSC and Euratom merge to become the European Community.
1972	Beginning of Community environmental policy.

Date	Events
1973	UK, Ireland and Denmark join the Community. Norway rejects membership.
1975	British people accept re-negotiated terms of entry to the Community in a referendum. Lomé Convention signed between the Community and forty-six nations in Africa, the Caribbean and the Pacific. Regional Fund comes into operation.
1978	A European Monetary System (EMS) established.
1979	First direct elections to the European Parliament, which then rejects the Community budget.
1981	Greece joins the Community.
1984	Second elections for the European Parliament. Agreement reached over Britain's contribution to the Community budget.
1985	The Commission proposes full economic union by 1992.
1986	The Community imposes limited economic sanctions on South Africa.
1987	The Community and Comecon formally recognize each other. Single European Act comes into force, preparing the way for a true common market by 1992.
1988	A Court of First Instance established.
1989	Third elections for the European Parliament.

Glossary

Balance of power	With no single state having dominance.
Budget	A statement of proposed taxation and expenditure.
Capitalism	An economic theory that believes in the virtue of free enterprise, and the right to individual property and wealth.
CFCs	Chlorofluorocarbons: man-made gases, used as propellants and in refrigeration, which break down into destructive gases in the stratosphere.
Collaborate	To work jointly with someone or something else.
Comecon	The Eastern European trading bloc.
Commission	The EC's civil service and main organ of government.
Convention	A tradition.
Council of Ministers	The EC's decision-making body.
Currency	The money of a country.
Decision	EC law which applies to some member states.
Directive	EC law which is left to individual states to administer as they wish.
Disarmament	Getting rid of military weapons.
EC	The European Community.
ECSC	The European Coal and Steel Community.
ECU	The European Currency Unit.
EEC	The European Economic Community.
EFTA	The European Free Trade Association.
Empire	Widespread territory controlled by a single government.
Euratom	The European Atomic Energy Commission.
Excise	Tax raised on goods manufactured within a single country.
Fluorocarbons	Inert gases used, for example, in refrigerators and aerosols.
Fusion	Joining together.
Gross Domestic Product (GDP)	Annual total value of goods produced and services provided in a country.
Heritage	The traditions that a country inherits from its past.
Inflation	When money loses its value and prices rise.
Inherent	Built-in, permanent.
Isolationist	Unwilling to enter into agreements with other nations.
Legislation	Laws.
Levy	Tax.
MEP	A member of the European Parliament.
Migrant	Moving from one state or area to another.
NATO	The North Atlantic Treaty Organization, a defensive alliance of Western nations.
OEEC	The Organization of European Economic Co-operation.
Quota	A fixed share.
Referendum	A popular poll, in which people get a chance to vote for or against a proposal.

Reformation	The movement that split Christendom into Roman Catholic and Protestant Churches in the sixteenth century.
Refugees	People who, owing to religious or political persecution, seek refuge in a foreign country.
Regulation	EC law binding on all member states.
Socialism	An economic theory which believes that the state should own all important means of the production and distribution of wealth.
Sovereignty	Supreme power.
Statesman	A politician of international reputation.
Summit	A meeting of heads of state or other high-ranking government officials.
Surplus	That which is left over. Amount that is in excess of what is required.
Tariffs	Tax on goods passing from one country to another.
The Continent	The European states.
The Six	The original nations who signed the Treaty of Rome: France, Germany, Italy, Luxembourg, the Netherlands and Belgium.
Third World	The non-industrialized, developing nations of the world.
Unanimous	With no disagreement.
VAT	Value Added Tax.
Veto	The right to stop decisions and actions being carried out.
Warsaw Pact	The European communist military alliance.

Further reading

There are not many books on the European Community suitable for school use. But the Community itself publishes hundreds of leaflets, pamphlets, booklets and full length works, a list of which can be found in *The European Community as a Publisher* (European Community, Luxembourg, updated annually). Further information can be obtained from the Information Office of the European Communities, 8 Storey's Gate, London SW1P 3AT, tel: 01-222-8122.

Useful Community publications include:
A Journey Through the EC, 1986.
About Europe, 1987.
Britain, Europe, the World.
Europe Today: State of European Integration, 1983.
Europe Without Frontiers – Completing the Internal Market, 1988.
Europe in Figures, 1988.
European Unification – The Origins and Growth of the European Community, 1987.
The European Community: Who? What? Why? How? Where Does Britain Fit In?, 1986.
The European Parliament, 1987.
Learning About the European Community.
Noel, Emile, *Working Together: The Institutions of the European Community*, 1988.
Steps to European Unity, 1987.
Uniting Europe, 1987.
Women in the European Community, 1984.

Among other works are:
Barker, E., *Britain in a Divided Europe, 1945-70*, Weidenfeld & Nicolson, 1972.
Budd, S. A., *The EEC: A Guide to the Maze*, INRO Press, Edinburgh, 1985.
Haig, B., *A New Community in Europe*, Macdonald, 1985.
Gregory, P., *Britain and the EEC*, Martin Robertson, 1983.
Ross, Stewart, *The European Parliament*, Wayland, 1987.
Tugendhat, Christopher, *Making Sense of Europe*, Viking, 1986.

Particularly helpful are articles in *The Economist*, especially its monthly update of EC affairs. Other newspapers, magazines and journals run regular articles and features on the Community.

Notes on sources

1   Cited in John Bowle, *Western Political Thought*, Methuen, 1961, p.232.
2   D. Ogg, *Europe in the Seventeenth Century*, A & C Black, 1961, p.78.
3   William L. Shirer, *The Rise and Fall of the Third Reich*, Simon & Schuster, 1960, p.137.
4   *Steps to European Unity*, The European Communities, 1981, p.10.
5   *Chronicle of the Twentieth Century*, Longman, 1988, p.646.
6   *Uniting Europe*, The European Communities, 1982, p.5.
7   From *The Treaty of Paris*. It can be found, *inter alia*, in Stanley A. Budd, *The EEC: A Guide to the Maze*, INRO Press, 1985, pp.10–11.
8   From the Messina Declaration, June 1955, cited in *Uniting Europe, op.cit*, p.6.
9   *The Times*, 26 October 1971, p.13. (The tense has been altered to the present.)
10 *Ibid.*
11 *Ibid.*, 29 October 1971, p.7
12 *Ibid.*, 28 October 1971, p.13
13 *Ibid.*, 29 October 1971, p.6
14 From Budd, *op. cit*, p.16.
15 *Ten Years in the European Parliament 1973–1983*, The European Parliament Information Office, 1983, p.14.
16 *The Economist*, 3 December 1988, p.54.
    Ibid., 15 October 1988, p.66
18 *Britain, Europe, the World*, The European Commission, p.20.
19 Cited in the leaflet 'The European Parliament and the Rights of Women', the Directorate-General for Information and Public Relations, Luxembourg.
20 *European Parliament – The Week*, 12–16 December 1988, p.12.
21 *About Europe*, The European Commission, 1987, p.8.
22 *The Economist*, 17 December 1988, p.50.
23 *The Economist*, 17 September 1988, p.64.
24 1987 figures from *About Europe, op.cit.* pp.18–19.
25 *Ibid.* and *The European Community*, The Commission, p.24.
26 *The Economist*, 17 December 1988, p.50.
27 *The European Community, op.cit.* p.19.
28 *Twelve Nations One Parliament*, leaflet published by the European Parliament.
29 All figures from *About Europe, op.cit.* p.20, and the leaflet *The European Parliament and Foreign Trade*, The European Parliament.
30 Budd, *op.cit.* p.99.
31 *Ibid.*, p.100, and the leaflet *The European Parliament and the Third World*, The European Parliament.
32 *Europe Without Frontiers – Completing the Internal Market*, Luxembourg: Office for Official Publications of the Communities, 1988, p.7.
33 *The Economist*, 1 October 1988, p.62.
34 *Time*, 23 January 1989, p.8.

Picture acknowledgements

The author and publishers would like to thank the following for allowing their illustrations to be reproduced in this book: Camera Press Ltd 4, 5 (bottom), 10, 11, 13, 19, 31, 32, 39 (bottom), 40, 42, 45 (both), 46, 48, 49, 51; Garland, *Daily Telegraph* 18; Vicky, *Evening Standard* 20; Greenpeace 29; Rex Features 15, 23, 33, 35; Topham Picture Library 5 (top), 6, 8, 9 (both), 12, 16, 17, 21, 22, 24, 25, 28, 30, 34, 36, 39 (top), 41, 43 (both), 47, 50, 53, 54, 55; Wayland Picture Library 37. The maps and diagrams were supplied by Peter Bull. Thanks also to the Centre for the study of Cartoons and Caricature, University of Kent, Canterbury.

Index